TIRED OF BEING ...
STUCK?

IT'S TIME TO MINE YOUR GEMS

BY

MICHELE R. JONES

ISBN-13: 978-1974318322

ISBN-10: 197431832X

Dedication

This book is dedicated to:

The Gem Creator My Heavenly Father and His son, Jesus Christ

My Parents- Elaine R. Jones & John L. Jones

Beloved Sisters- Margarette Sinclair, Carol Feracho, Denise Perry-Eans & Sharon Wynn-Robles

My youth pastors Jerry & Mary June Lewin and young adult pastors Chris & Peg Rhone who helped identify and began mining the Gems out of me.

My local Pastors who encouraged me to stay in the fields these past sixteen years to keep mining for other Gems!

To God Be The Glory!

But we have this treasure in earthen vessels, that the excellency of the power may be of God, and not of us.

2 Corinthians 4:7 KJV

Table of Contents

Introduction

This book is written to you who feel STUCK! To you who are frustrated, feeling contained within a bottle sadly watching everyone else go by and also sick and tired of "going around the mountain" another time!

You try and try, yet you keep hitting that glass ceiling, you keep hitting that plateau, you keep stepping into the same "ditch" whether in your health, in your finances, ministry, business ventures or your relationships. You want to break out of the bottle, you want more, yet you wonder... "How do I accomplish it?!"

In this book you will receive 5 powerfully proven GEMS, which have TRANSFORMED the lives of people across the globe! Once acted upon, these GEMS enabled their lives to become UNSTUCK — from going around the mountain another time, from self-sabotage behavioral patterns, from feeling frustrated, from feeling isolated, from feeling a vulnerable victim and more.

Book Purpose

The purpose of this book is to help you become UNSTUCK in every area of your life by challenging you with proven principles that have transformed my life and countless others across the globe.

These GEMS will empower you to realize the freedom, personal goals, security and the dreams God placed in your heart. You will walk away with a solid plan of action.

You will learn how to turn your vision/dream into reality. And most of all you too will discover YOUR inner treasure!

There is Hope because you are not alone. We are in this together. You, were MADE for MORE!

Are you ready to become UNSTUCK?!

From The Nuthouse

Let me share with you the story of a woman who thought her dreams had come true only to watch them turn into a sad, painful nightmare of betrayal, isolation, fear of financial ruin, loss of self-worth, loss of social status, anger and distrust of those closest to her!

She became STUCK!

I was married at the age of 33. Up to that moment, my life included traveling, endeavoring to grow personally and in my uniqueness as a single Christian woman. I actively participated in my local church, had served as a missionary to inner cities, pursued the things of God for almost 10 years prior and led a weekly home Bible study group. Working hard and with the grace of God, I became quite successful in the corporate world, having access to company cars, extravagant expense accounts and traveling in first-class accommodations.

Eighteen months before meeting my future mate, I purchased my first home and excitedly looked forward to the prospect of decorating it.

Two months later, after I moved into the new house, my future husband and I were introduced at the checkout counter of a local home improvement store by a mutual acquaintance who happened to be working at the store that particular day.

The seed for a budding friendship was planted. Over the next three months we became inseparable. I enjoyed his sense of humor and relaxed style while he enjoyed my candid approach to life. Time passed, and I trusted him to dog sit for me. He would buy emergency groceries for me when I traveled, drop them off so I would return home to a stocked house.

One day he asked to attend church with me. This became a regular activity. He would pick me up on Sundays for church, and then, we'd spend the afternoon at lunch or visiting with other singles from the church. He became my guest on special corporate sponsored events. He was, now, my dear friend and companion.

We got married in the fall of the following year in a regal ceremony at a private manor hosted by my church, family and friends. The entire weekend was filled with dancing and celebration at our lively reception.

My in-laws gifted us a tropical honeymoon. Yet it was during the second evening of the honeymoon our relationship began to change. We were discussing how we plan to handle joint household responsibilities when we returned home from the trip. He shared how he had been experiencing some pain and physical discomfort from his current job. I asked him if he would consider changing professions.

He became enraged, cursed at me, walked away and then barely said two sentences to me during dinner. That evening he refused to allow me to touch him as he grabbed the sheets and turned his shoulder to me in bed.

This response was shocking and confusing as I'd never saw this harshness before! I had no idea this behavior could or would repeat itself over and over and escalate from this point.

The next few years became a pattern of good days followed by days when he felt offended and "punished" me by not speaking to me.

He would leave the house for days at a time without telling me where he was going. He insisted if I wanted to contact him, I'd have to call his pager.

I'd apologize after these episodes; then, he would respond with a card and flowers. This became a destructive "going around the mountain" cycle that grew more frequent.

After we were married, the affection level suddenly began to drop yet while he courted me showing affection or simple hand holding was not a concern. Our core issues were questions on various levels of intimacy. I wanted to know why he couldn't or would no longer treat me in a wifely manner and each time he responded, "You're becoming too needy or that's just not me."

With a burning desire to maintain our marriage, I was receptive to doing whatever was necessary to please him. I went on a quest to "lose weight" (even though I was at the ideal body frame level), began working out, changed my hairstyles and even changed mannerisms to become "the" woman he needed and desired.

I was now actively (yet unknown to me at the time) in the characterized domestic abuse "crazy-making" cycle. I had lost all sense of "self" to please him.

Initially, he refused counseling, so I began marital counseling on my own. Searching and seeking to discover how to become a better wife, how to change my personality and how to be willing to do whatever he asked me to do.

During our third separation, he contacted me severely sick with the flu and asked me to bring him home. (I had no idea where he had been staying the past two weeks.)

When he gave me the address, I was shocked to discover it was less than 2 miles away from our home. This meant he was driving past our house every day to and from work!

I picked him up, helped him change clothes and stayed by the shower to make sure he didn't lose his balance and fall. Afterwards, I helped him get back into bed.

The next two days I fed him soup. He even cuddled under me while he slept. On the third day, I returned home from work. The house was quiet; I crept in slowly so I wouldn't disturb him. Walking into the bedroom, I found the bed neatly made with no sign of him anywhere.

I searched the house: his den, the kitchen, everywhere and then, I spotted a note on the dining room table.

Reading the words, "Thanks feeling better went back to my buddy's house," I was devastated! I sat there in shock and cried; I balled up the note and threw it across the room.

It finally clicked in my head, "He had no desire to respect our marriage vows or to work through our problems." Slowly I took off my clothes. All the energy drained from my bones from crying. I changed into my nightgown and crawled into bed.

I stayed there for two days, feeling numb, slipping into depression and hopelessness. Helpless and cornered in with no place to go and no hope for change in sight —

I felt STUCK!

During our final year of marriage, my husband only allowed me to contact him by way of his pager.

Discussions for any further steps to save our marriage would be under his terms only, ignoring the terms of our various pastoral counselors. Separated again and with no mutual desire for change, I weighed the matter in prayer with further spiritual counsel. I took account of my remaining "threads" of self-respect and sanity then notified him of my decision to file for divorce.

I shared I was unable to continue a union under these conditions and from that point he made no further attempts for reconciliation. Even on the final day of the divorce proceedings, the judge extended our time on the docket, I waited anxiously outside of the courtroom for him to appear, hoping for any glimmer of reconciliation. Yet, he chose not to appear.

My dreams and hopes were shattered...

I felt STUCK!

I was STUCK. My dreams of a Godly marriage and family were gone! As a leader in our local church, I now felt ostracized. Members did not know how to make eye contact or speak with me, and I stopped holding Bible studies in my home. Feeling like a failure and an embarrassment to my family, friends (who looked up to me) and most of all to God, the feelings were overpowering.

I fell into depression of anger and disappointment. I was angry at the situation, angered that "the charming wolf" got past my family, friends and pastors and angry at God!

Lord, I "thought" I knew you, **HOW** did this thing get through? Going to my corporate job during the day wearing "a smile mask," I would quickly retreat at home to my bed and crawl into a fetal position until the next morning! I stopped answering the ringing phone calls from family and friends. I sought to erase the painful memories, made the hard decision to sell the home, sadly give away our two show dogs to a local adoption shelter and was inspired to give away most of the furniture, as a blessing, to the other couples in our church.

I moved to a quaint 2-bedroom apartment in the neighboring state with my Bible, books, a dining table and an air mattress.

To The White House

During the last transport of belongings from the house to the apartment, I was so overcome with grief and depression. While driving on the highway towards the Woodrow Wilson bridge, a voice said, "Just drive off; Your pain will be gone. Just do it!"

Tears were streaming down my face, my vision become blurred, I struggled to stay within the white lines and felt myself moving towards the railing to drive off the 70-foot high drawbridge.

I cried out, "Lord, help me!" At that very moment, I heard a still small voice say, "Daughter, you shall live and NOT die. You shall declare my praises. I am bringing you to a place of rest."

The steering wheel seemed to move in the opposite direction as I held on, and by God's grace He saved me from any car accidents on this six-lane drawbridge. I drove into the next state with tears running down my face, but now a quiet peace in my heart.

In that sweet apartment, I slept on the air mattress for over six months, and I began to find God's peace again!

He tenderly mined priceless GEMS from His Word back into the depths of my heart. Through the painful healing process from the loss of our marriage, God literally rebuilt my heart from the inside out and made it BRAND NEW! The very God I was earlier "upset" with was the same loving God who healed my heart when I cried out and returned to Him! What an AMAZING love?!

"Arise [from spiritual depression to a new life], shine [be radiant with the glory and brilliance of the Lord]; for your light has come, And the glory and brilliance of the Lord has risen upon you."

Isaiah 60:1AMP

In 1999, after the restoration, God called me to leave the corporate world to take the notes and teachings He spoke to my heart to now help other women also MINE their God-given worth with the truths of Jesus Christ!

I was inspired to share my journal notes with my new local church in a meeting with the Director of Counseling. The meeting was scheduled for thirty minutes. We prayed. She read my notes then caught her breath. We ended almost ninety minutes later!

She exclaimed, "Wow, we have a sea of women coming through with the painful effects of abuse, and it appears God has given you keys to help them! Let me talk with our senior leadership and make them aware of your program notes. It may take some time, yet let me get back to you."

Two months later I was invited to start the first class to help women heal from the effects of dating/domestic abuse. The first class launched in April 2001 with twelve hurting women and their children!

Since 2001, dozens and dozens of women enrolled, and have gone through the biblically based program, we soon became a non-profit organization. In 2006, as founder and President of our non-profit I was honored to be invited to the White House as one of a select group of nationwide faith-based leaders to witness the President instituting the "Violence Against Women Act!"

We were commended by The President of The United States for making a positive impact in seeing families restored from the pain of domestic abuse. Over a span of fifteen years, God has opened the door to allow me to share these proven GEM principles to be recognized on the federal, state, local and international levels as an effective model in now helping countless others become UNSTUCK!

"As for you, you meant evil against me, but God meant it for good in order to bring about this present outcome, that many people would be kept alive [as they are this day]."

Genesis 50:20 AMP

God certainly has a sense of ironic humor! The very "behavioral enemy" that almost took my life mentally, emotionally, physically, and financially; God was now using me to declare His triumphant power and victory over it!

Only He can take you from a STUCK situation, heal your heart, heal your mind, clean you off and give you purpose solely for His glory.

Why?

So that HE may SHINE through — you!

I've now taught hundreds of women from every walk of life, every educational and socioeconomic level, have spoken nationally and internationally on HOW to mine your gems. They are now living their individual dreams of healthy relationships, owning businesses, launching ministries/non-profits, governing entities and MORE! When life does throw curve balls they now also have the tools to get UNSTUCK!

As you apply them, you too will become:

◈ Encouraged

◈ Enlightened

◈ Empowered

Now, let's get started!

Stuck Signs

You know you are STUCK when:

◈ You continue making the same choices and getting the same disappointing outcomes.

◈ You "think" you've changed yet you continue reacting the same way in given situations or circumstances. The same self - defeating behavioral patterns emerge.

◈ You believe you can "change" someone else.

◈ Your dream or vision in your heart you long, anticipate and await has dried up and fallen by the wayside.

◈ Your expectation you envisioned taking you onward and upward sadly crashes flat, leaving you feeling hopeless.

◈ The desire of performing "perfectly" and/ or the fear of "failure" can paralyze you from moving forward

◈ Instead of taking you upward, something goes terribly wrong where you now feel broken, frustrated and confused. You may feel God has abandoned you, while leaving you seething in a pool of anger!

◈ You are seeking approval or acceptance from a multitude of others before taking any action

◈ You keep talking about your dream/vision, yet no action has taken place.

This book will highlight five of fifteen GEMS that initially helped move me forward. And, in time over a span of sixteen years, I was able to show countless others **HOW to also become UNSTUCK!**

 *"The wealthiest places in the world are not gold mines, oil fields, diamond mines or banks. The wealthiest place is the cemetery. There lies companies that were never started, masterpieces that were never painted... In the cemetery there is buried the greatest treasure of untapped potential. There is a treasure within you that must come out. Don't go to the grave with your treasure still within YOU."*

~Dr. Myles Munroe

GEM FACT

DIAMONDS
ARE
HIDDEN

GEM 1: It Starts With A Choice

Are you READY and WILLING to become UNSTUCK?

Are you sick and tired of being sick and tired?

It starts with a CHOICE and only YOU can answer the question.

"When Jesus noticed him lying there [helpless], knowing that he had already been a long time in that condition, He said to him, Do you want to become well?
[Are you really in earnest about getting well?]"

John 5:6 AMPC

Let's discuss some historical records of men and women who seriously desired to become UNSTUCK.

Each had a different area (in life) where they were STUCK. And, they all had one thing in common.

What was it?

Jesus Christ came to heal and set you free from every bondage attempting to enslave you by your choice or the poor choices of others made upon you.

This healing includes: mental, emotional, physical, sexual, financial, relational, generational, spiritual bondage and everything attempting to hold you back from being all that you can be in this life! (Isaiah 61: 1)

◈ **The woman with the twelve-year-old issue (Mark 5:24-34)** She had an issue for so long it drained all her financial and emotional resources while searching for recovery the world's way. She became a social outcast, destined to live a lonely life. Her quest only ended with her condition becoming worse! How much time and money have you invested seeking help yet the situation has only gotten worse and left in a worse position than when you started?

◈ **The invalid of 38 years (John 5:2-14)** Sometimes we, too become invalids by not exercising our free will. We passively lay there in a perceived helpless condition allowing life to happen to us. We become a victim in our own minds. Jesus challenged this man, "ARE YOU SERIOUS ABOUT GETTING WELL?" He is asking YOU the same question today.

◈ **The Blind Beggar (Mark 10:46-52, Luke 18:35-42)** This man was blind and a beggar. Society discounted him, walked by him and attempted to silence him. Some of us are STUCK because we are blind. Our blindness allows us to keep stepping into the same ditch of life and receiving the same poor results! Family, friends and the world have discounted you and even attempted to silence your voice. Today, Jesus asks the same question of you, "WHAT DO YOU WANT ME TO DO FOR YOU?". The blind man wanted to become unstuck. He was SPECIFIC, "I want my sight!". You, too, can be specific with Jesus Christ. Simply, tell Him what you want!

◈ **The woman who was crippled for over 18 years by demonic spirits (Luke 13:11-17)** Some of us are bound up, STUCK by demonic influence. Sadly, similar as this woman, it can bow you over, give you a distorted view of life and cause you to become the center of others jokes. This woman was unable to make eye contact with anyone nor enjoy her life because she suffered from the bent condition for eighteen years. Jesus Christ saw the true nature of her situation, had compassion for the woman and understood her pain and shame. Christ understands your shame, your pain and where you're unable to make eye contact with the world He declares to you, "TODAY YOU ARE SET FREE FROM YOUR INFIRMITY!"

◈ **Childhood Issues (Mark 9:17-24)** Some of us are stuck because of something originating in our childhood, and it still negatively controls your adult life. An example is the lunatic boy's condition, which would bring him harm by throwing the boy into fires with seizures. Unresolved childhood issues can bring harm to you and distress to your family members who are helplessly watching the dangerous effects. Jesus Christ says, *"All things are possible to those who believe,"* and the boy was healed according to the father's belief. The question is still the same today, "WILL YOU BELIEVE?!"

These people came from varying walks of life, different socioeconomic levels with different challenging long-term conditions. Their common denominators:

Each cried out to Christ and believed He could heal them, He alone could set them free and each received healing.

Each also received healing according to their expectation; they made the choice, took the corresponding action and said "YES" I want to become unstuck.

Each declared in their heart and mind, "I WANT TO BE HEALED, I WANT TO BE MADE WELL!"

"And He said to her, Daughter, your faith (your confidence and trust in Me) has made you well! Go(enter) into peace (untroubled, undisturbed well-being)."

Luke 8:48 AMPC

Make the Gem choice today to become UNSTUCK as you declare:

"I AM SERIOUS AND EARNEST ABOUT GETTING WELL!"

GEM 1 Gift Box

We must first begin to shine light on the dark place(s). Please print your GEM sheet.

Go to below link to open and receive your gift! (http://www.miningforgems.com/gem-1-gift/) (Gift Value of $150)

Coaching Tip: You now have your target(s) for specific action to begin!

My GEM 1 Reflections

Tired of Being... Stuck?

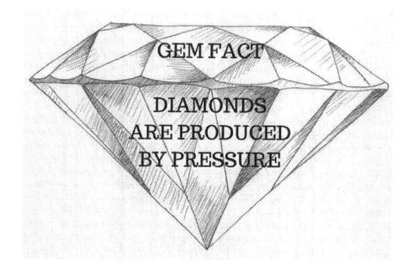

GEM FACT

DIAMONDS
ARE PRODUCED
BY PRESSURE

GEM 2: The Art of Receiving

When you are STUCK you don't know HOW to properly ask!

"Up to this time you have not asked a [single] thing in my name [that is, presenting all I Am] but now ask and keep on asking and you will receive, so that your joy (gladness, delight) may be full and complete"

John 16:24 AMPC

God is a Giver of GOOD gifts! He can only give Who He is.

Here we see three points in the equation:

1. **Who Are You Asking For Help?** Jesus stated up to this point they had NOT asked Him a single thing in His Name or recognize His authority to answer the request. Today, He challenges you to stop going to family, friends or anyone else for counsel for your needs. He wants you to know the door is open wide for you to confidently come directly to Him.

2. **He told them to ASK and keep on ASKING.** Some of us are challenged in asking due to responses we experienced in the past from people. We've received rejection, apathy or were expected to receive with "strings attached." Others grew independent of caregivers and have "vowed" of ourselves to NEVER ask. Some of us were never taught how to receive anything from anyone! Finally pride and our own expectations of HOW God is "supposed to deliver the response" could allow us to actually miss the answer God wants to bring into our lives! For example, let's look at a high ranking military official named Naaman who almost missed receiving his healing from leprosy because the

answer did not come the way he thought or expected! His pride and presumption nearly stopped him from receiving God's answer to his problem. (2 Kings 5: 1- 13 NIV)

"Now Naaman was commander of the army of the king of Aram. He was a great man in the sight of his master and highly regarded, because through him the LORD had given victory to Aram. He was a valiant soldier, but he had leprosy."

2 Kings 5:1 NIV

"But Naaman went away angry and said, "I thought he would surely come out to me and stand and call on the name of the Lord his God, wave his hand over the spot and cure me of my leprosy. Are not Abana and Pharpar, the rivers of Damascus, better than all the waters of Israel? Could'nt I wash in them and be cleansed?" So he turned and went off in a rage."

2 Kings 5:11,12 NIV

When you ask, God challenges you to take the limitations, preconceived thoughts and expectations OFF of how He chooses to respond. Why? Because

He can do exceedingly, abundantly above however you can ask, think, dream or imagine!

> *"Now to Him Who, by (in consequence of) the [action of His] power that is at work within us, is able to [carry out His purpose and] do superabundantly, far over and above all that we [dare] ask or think [infinitely beyond our highest prayers, desires, thoughts, hopes, or dreams]*

Ephesians 3:20 AMPC

God wants you to begin asking HIM, and He wants you to be willing to continue asking Him! It's a shift for one to make especially if you think God is "too busy or doesn't care about the size of your matter." God DOES desire for us to learn to ask boldly of Him. Why? He knows the frailty of human nature. People can easily miss our expectations and disappoint us, yet God will not!

Today, God encourages you to shift gears and raise your EXPECTATION. He hears you and is ready, willing and able to supply your need.

> *"Keep on asking and it will be given you; [b]keep on seeking and you will find; [c]keep on knocking [reverently] and [the door] will be opened to you.*

For everyone who keeps on asking receives; and he who keeps on seeking finds; and to him who keeps on knocking, [the door] will be opened"

Matt 7:7-8 AMPC

"And my God will liberally supply (fill to the full) your every need according to His riches in glory in Christ Jesus."

Phil 4:19 AMPC

3. Then, He told them to **RECEIVE** that their joy may be FULL! Do you know HOW to receive? Some of us have received a gift, yet we NEVER opened it because we felt unworthy or ashamed to fully embrace the gift. God wants you to be free to EMBRACE His gifts and to OPEN them — use it and enjoy!

"If you then, evil as you are, know how to give good and advantageous gifts to your children, how much more will your Father Who is in heaven [perfect as He is] give good and advantageous things to those who keep on asking Him!"

Matthew 7:11 AMPC

Now, read each of the following words carefully, and I encourage you to speak each action out loud.

As a giver of good gifts, God's desire is for us to **ask** Him, to **receive** it (to take it within our hands), **hold** onto it, **receive it in our hearts**, then **open it** up AND **open it up with an expectation** that it is GOOD! He desires for YOUR joy to be made full.

God wants to respond! He's ready willing and able!

If necessary — write down your specific requests on a piece of paper, thank Him for the answers, hold it up in the air and say, "God, I thank you for the answers in your perfect timing and your perfect way! I expect it! I receive it! In Jesus Name. Amen"

It's a NEW day. Regardless of your past circumstances and responses from others you have a **new day** before you.

Become UNSTUCK today.

It only requires one thing. You must be willing to receive. You don't have to give anything. Yes, today open your arms WIDE and choose to RECEIVE from Him!

GEM 2 Gift Box

Discover your unique personality and receiving style:

◈ How do you relate to people?

◈ How do you interact with the others?

Go to below link to open and receive your gift! (http://www.miningforgems.com/gem-2-gift/) (Gift Value of $225)

You're welcome to Email Results To:

info@miningforgems.com

Coaching Tip: Let's take a moment to identify any barriers which may hinder your receiving.

My GEM 2 Reflections

GEM 3: The Valley of Indecision

When you are STUCK, it is extremely challenging to make decisions.

Yet, straddling in between "two opinions" will only torment your mind and keep you unstable. Satan enjoys keeping you in the "valley of indecision". Doubt, worry, fear and procrastination are the main drivers of indecision.

"[For being as he is] a man of two minds (hesitating, dubious, irresolute), [he is] unstable and unreliable and uncertain about everything [he thinks, feels, decides]."

James 1:8 AMPC

God has an answer for you.

"Elijah came near to all the people, and said, „How long will you halt and limp between two opinions? If the Lord is God, follow Him! But if Baal, then follow him." And the people did not answer him a word."

I Kings 18:21 AMPC

How to become UNSTUCK?

I challenge you right now with these steps:

A. Take out two sheets of paper. On the first sheet write at the top: "WHAT COULD GO WRONG". On the second sheet write on the top "WITH GOD ALL THINGS ARE POSSIBLE/ WHAT CAN GO RIGHT!" If necessary, after you have written them down, then speak out loud the options you noted on both sides.

B. Write down how you would like your life to change within 30, 60, 90 days and a 6-month time frame.

Envision it and begin to write down what you see: your health, relationships, career, finances, education and more.

"Then the Lord answered me and said, "Write the vision And engrave it plainly on [clay] tablets. So that the one who reads it will run."

Habakkuk 2:2 AMP

This action will begin to bring clarity and direction beyond your present circumstance.

C. Next, get an accountability partner — someone who can help inspire you to move forward without taking excuses. Determine to address at least 1 goal per week and check in with your accountability partner.

Today, God asks you the same question:

How long will you waiver between two opinions?

When I was inspired to start a faith-based program to help women overcome abuse, I struggled between staying in a six-figure corporate position and day dreaming of the possibility of helping others. Three months later, after much prayer and accountability from family and closest friends, I wrote my resignation letter to step out to answer the strong prompting within my heart! I said, "God help me trust You with your guidance, because I don't want to be 90 years old wondering what would have happened if I had followed the vision!"

I turned in my resignation letter on a Monday; despite two counter offers from corporate, I stepped out of the boat giving a 30-day notice and offer of training any potential candidates. I asked, He answered…then I had to respond. The straddling was over. Peace came over my heart and mind. I was now…UNSTUCK!

As we discovered in GEM 2, begin to ASK of God for His guidance and direction. Whatever He tells you to do, DO IT! His answer will clear the path of confusion and bring you peace. God wants to set you FREE to become UNSTUCK He alone knows where He wants to take your life for His glory. Trust Him to navigate you safely through to the other side!

"When you walk, they will guide you; when you sleep, they will watch over you; when you awake, they will speak to you. For this command is a lamp, this teaching is a light, and correction and instruction are the way to life," Proverbs 6:22,23 NIV

Take The Three Steps Towards Becoming … UNSTUCK!

My GEM 3 Reflections

Tired of Being... Stuck?

GEM FACT

A DIAMOND
MUST BE
CUT TO DISPLAY
ITS BEAUTY

GEM 4: Take Off the Velcro Suit

You are STUCK when you keep talking about the same issues long past the time of the occurrence. This means it's time to resolve past issues that are attempting to STICK to you from month to month or unfortunately tormenting others from year to year!

You KNOW "those people," when you see them coming you just want to run and hide! Why? You know within minutes of the start of the conversation they will be telling you the SAME story (you can even fill in the lines for them because you have heard it over and over).

It seems as though they are "frozen" in time with the offense. Whether it was months ago or YEARS ago, they recount the details with such vitality one would think it occurred moments ago!

Velcro "stickies" cling to you like a cactus ball on the hem of your pants! They include: shame, guilt, condemnation, anger, bitterness, resentment, unforgiveness and offense. These behavioral responses and mindsets will keep you going around the mountain over and over until you make a choice to resolve them!

The deceptive design of these "prickly" behaviors solely hinders YOU from moving forward and becoming the powerful person God destined.

In Psalms 103:2-4,11,12, God declares, when you go to Him, He forgives all your iniquities, He takes back your life from the pit and destruction then He beautifies and dignifies your life with loving kindness.

Similar to those painful sticky cactus balls you want to learn to shake off guilt, condemnation, and unrighteousness they just keep you STUCK! God forgives and pardons you when you ask for it.

If God forgives you, isn't it time for you to forgive and forget the offenses too?

"He then goes on to say, And their sins and their lawbreakings

I will remember no more."

Hebrews 10:17 AMPC

Here's your practical exercise: Write down two lists. First, list where YOU have offended God. On the second, list write down where OTHERS have offended you. Then prayerfully submit both lists to God. How?

1. On the first list — Ask for God's forgiveness where you have offended Him!

"If we [freely] admit that we have sinned and confess our sins, He is faithful and just [true to His nature and promises] and will forgive our sins (dismiss our lawlessness) and continuously cleanse us from all unrighteousness everything not in conformity to His will in purpose, thought and action."

I John 1:9 AMPC

You can pour out your heart before God because He is never shocked by our outbursts towards others or Him! In fact, He already knows. By opening up, you are saying to Him and to yourself, "God, I trust you."

"Come now, and let us reason together, says the Lord; though your sins be as scarlet, they shall be as white as snow; though they be red like crimson, they shall be as wool."

Isaiah 1:18 AMPC

The moment you decide to repent and ask for the Lord's forgiveness, He cleanses you of all your past sins and transgressions. Bring your sins to Jesus Christ. He alone can save and completely free you from a "stained" past (Hebrews 7:25)!

2. On the second list ask God for the grace to RELEASE the offenders and situations on that list to Him. Why? His shoulders are bigger as your Burden Bearer and His justice is Righteous in restoring His people.

"And whenever you stand praying, if you have anything against any one, forgive him and let it drop leave it, let it go— in order that your Father Who is in Heaven may also forgive you your [own] failings and shortcomings and let them drop. But if you do not forgive, neither will your Father in heaven forgive your failings and shortcomings."

Mark 11:25, 26 AMPC

Lack of forgiveness actually produces a "tormenting weight" of oppression and a "prickliness" within your soul. It prevents you from enjoying other relationships in life (family, friends, co-workers, etc.). Most importantly, you won't enjoy your relationship with your Heavenly Father.

Imagine yourself tying a chain around your neck, yet you expect the "unforgiven" person to choke! This is unreasonable, yet we do this every day. You're the one holding onto unforgiveness, your mind keeps replaying the offense and your life becomes tangled in messy knots.

Meanwhile, the unsuspecting "unforgiven" person is moving on, enjoying their life. They're totally unaware or unconcerned about the thoughts you're holding against them. You have now choked up your mind and life while they're the "happy campers moving freely about the cabin"!

Is this sound logic to you?

Now YOU are the only one who is STUCK.

"For we know Him Who said, Vengeance is Mine—
retribution and the meting out of full justice rest with Me; I
will repay I will exact the compensation, says the Lord. And
again, The Lord will judge and determine and solve and settle
the cause and the cases of His people.
It is a fearful (formidable and terrible) thing to incur the
divine penalties and be cast into the hands of the living God!"
Hebrews 10:30,31 AMPC

I can recall the day when The Lord spoke to my heart through His Word, "Daughter if I can forgive you when you cry out and repent, can you not trust me to resolve the pain, disappointment, injustice and offense of the relationship?" I said, "Yes, Lord, help me to trust YOU!" I wrote a letter to my then ex-husband sharing where I forgave him, where God has challenged ME to grow and most of all wishing him well in wherever life takes him. I said a prayer of release to give the entire moment and matter to God. Within seconds of finishing the prayer and dropping the letter into the mailbox...I felt a WEIGHT LIFT off of me that I didn't realize was resting upon my soul! I felt like a school girl wanting to skip home from the mailbox back to the apartment! **Forgiveness is about releasing YOU and allowing YOU to be free.** The great deception exists when you unknowingly (or foolishly) think it's about the other person!!! God wants you to move on, enjoy your life, and allow Him to deal with the offender.

God will be the One to repay for anyone's injustice! In the meantime, Choose to Live in Peace

"Repay no one evil for evil, but take thought for what is honest and proper and noble aiming to be above reproach in the sight of every one. If possible, as far as it depends on you, live at peace with every one.

Beloved, never avenge yourselves, but leave the way open for [God's] wrath; for it is written, Vengeance is Mine, I will repay (requite), says the Lord.

But, if your enemy is hungry, feed him; if he is thirsty, give him drink; for by so doing you will heap burning coals upon his head.

Do not let yourself be overcome by evil, but overcome (master) evil with good."

Romans 12:17-21 AMPC

Your time on earth is precious. Each day we must choose to use our time wisely to maximize our remaining moments on earth. Or, we choose to waste it entrapped in the snare of unforgiveness.

In Romans 12:18, the Lord directs us to live in peace as much as lies within our responsibility. Instead of repaying evil with evil, we are instructed to walk on the higher ground and do the noble thing.

Know that God fairly administers justice for injustices. Your relationships can also improve when you choose to do good towards those who have offended you. Your kind ways can cause them to warm up and you will overcome evil.

Time to Take Off The Velcro Suit!
Become...UNSTUCK!

My GEM 4 Reflections

GEM 4 Gift Box

Receive a FREE 30 minute personalized UNSTUCK strategy coaching session

Coaching Tip: Receive coaching to help identify your initial three practical steps to become UNSTUCK!

Limited spots available schedule your spot now: http://tinyurl.com/freeunstuckcoaching

(Value $500)

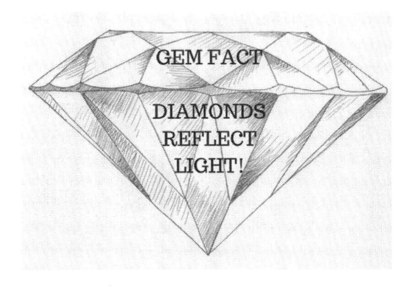

GEM FACT

DIAMONDS
REFLECT
LIGHT!

GEM 5: Just a Pitstop

When you are STUCK you feel "your life is **over,** this is the script I've **been dealt** I feel **hopeless** and **nothing** will change!"

Don't you dare put a "period" where God has only put a "comma" or "pregnant pause" at this moment of your life. Recognize this is just a pitstop NOT your destination!

Pitstops are required in all aspects of life. Timeouts are called in football and basketball games to allow athletes to relax, regroup and connect with their coach or trainer. NASCAR needs pitstops to refuel, change tires and make tweaks. A coach will call an athlete over to sit out on the bench to recharge, refocus and be redirected before putting them back on the field. We all need pitstops. Be encouraged, you are STILL in the game! You cannot run the obstacle course of life without moments to catch your breath, to learn, to tweak, and to reconnect with your coach.

"Do not [earnestly] remember the former things, neither consider the things of old.

Behold, I am doing a new thing; now it springs forth; do you not perceive and know it, and will you not give heed to it? I will make a way in the wilderness and rivers in the desert."

Isaiah 43:18,19 AMPC

God wants you to know TODAY: He is doing a new thing in your life! He is clearing a path for you and is bringing life into a former "dead" situation. Today, He is here tenderly taking and lifting your face upward into His hands.

The question is: will you cooperate with Him by walking in the NEW direction He has foreordained for your life?

"Arise [from spiritual depression to a new life], shine [be radiant with the glory and brilliance of the Lord]; for your light has come, And the glory and brilliance of the Lord has risen upon you."

Isaiah 60:1 AMPC

When the Lord told me, "Arise, Michele, this is a new day. Lift up your head. I have taken the things of the past away!" I realized that it was up to me to cooperate with His command. On that day, I made the commitment to God that I agreed...TODAY is the FIRST day of the rest of my life! I will no longer dwell on old thoughts, memories, and regrets, but I choose today to step into a "new day" for the next phase of my life!

"And I will restore or replace for you the years that the locust has eaten, the hopping locust, the stripping locust, and the crawling locust, My great army which I sent among you. And you shall eat in plenty and be satisfied, and praise the name of the Lord, your God, Who has dealt wondrously with you. And My people shall never be put to shame."

Joel 2:25,26 AMPC

From that day forward, the Lord brought a fresh wind through my soul, strengthened my heart, and set my mind free of the past. He will do the SAME for you if you will allow Him, and when you choose to cooperate with His plan.

"When you pass through the waters, I will be with you; and when you pass through the rivers, they will not sweep over you. When you walk through the fire, you will not be burned; the flames will not set you ablaze."

Isaiah 43:2 NIV

Remember you are passing **through**, this is just a pitstop **NOT** a final destination!

Due to His compassion, the Lord gives you a new start EACH day!

Why choose to hold onto stale, dead, or former things (old thoughts, responses, behaviors)?

"They are new every morning; great and abundant is Your stability and faithfulness."

Lamentations 3:23 AMPC

This can be the FIRST day of the rest of your life, apply each brilliant Gem and you too, with God's help can make a choice to become UNSTUCK!

After personally overcoming bullying, racism, sexism, cancer scares, near fatal car accidents, learning to walk again, having my head shaved from glass fragments about my face and head, depression, suicidal thoughts, personal/business financial comebacks, betrayal of close associates, loss of self esteem, isolation, being ostracized and an emotionally abusive marriage that ended in divorce, I know God is **NOT** a respecter of persons. Each time when life attempts to get us down, the HELP of God's Hand will pull you up to again move forward!

If I allowed myself to stay at the PITSTOP, I would certainly not have the privilege today to share with YOU! The depression, the weariness and the suicide were speaking, "It's too painful...your life will never change... get it over with NOW!"

But, the grace of God pours new mercies out upon our lives. The same painful life experience God actually used it to catapult me over the years to encourage, inspire, coach and challenge others around the world to trust HIM! As the saying goes "Let your TEST become your TESTIMONY." Allow God to help you pass your time of testing.

"You intended to harm me, but God intended it for good to accomplish what is now being done, the saving of many lives."
Genesis 50:20 NIV

He dug me OUT of the dark hole, He cleaned me off, He polished the rough places, and He cut off the dead places within my heart so that HE may shine. He can do the same for you IF you too allow Him.

"Surely the arm of the Lord is not too short to save, nor his ear too dull to hear."

Isaiah 59:1 NIV

"The steps of a [good] man are directed and established by the Lord, when He delights in his way [and He busies Himself with his every step]. Though he fall, he shall not be utterly cast down, for the Lord grasps his hand in support and upholds him."

Psalm 37:23,24 AMPC

Be encouraged today!

Declare today, "This is JUST a PITSTOP to my ordained DESTINATION!

Become...UNSTUCK!

My GEM 5 Reflections

"The more the diamond is cut the brighter it sparkles; and in what seems hard dealing, there God has no end in view but to perfect His people."

~Thomas Guthrie

GEM Recap

You now have in your hand five POWERFUL GEMS that have transformed the lives of thousands of people around the world and will do the same for you too! They now have dynamic healthy relationships, new business ventures, growing ministries, producing creative arts such as books, music and Christian productions and more!

God is **NO** respecter of persons what He's done for others He WILL do for you when we make the choice to apply the truths of His Word.

You have discovered:

◈ How To Recognize When YOU Are Stuck!

◈ Gem 1: It Starts With A Choice to Becoming Unstuck

◈ Gem 2: The Art Of Receiving and How To Begin Receiving

◈ Gem 3: The Valley Of Indecision and how to Climb Out

◈ Gem 4: Take Off The Velcro Suit So You May Become FREE To Move Forward!

◆ Gem 5: Just A Pitstop, This Is Simply A Testing And Resting Place Before God Moves You Onward

You've also received tools to identify where you are stuck and why; and uncovered your unique receiving personality. God's desire is to get you UNSTUCK so you may begin to fulfill the purpose He has planned for your life. Now it's up to YOU to do the work by applying what you have learned.

"Your eyes saw my unformed body; all the days ordained for me were written in your book before one of them came to be."

Psalm 139:16

"For I know the plans I have for you," declares the Lord "plans to prosper you and not to harm you, plans to give you hope and a future. "

Jeremiah 29:11

GEM Principles

◈ Diamonds are Hidden

◈ Diamonds are produced by Pressure

◈ Diamonds must be Cleaned Off

◈ Diamonds must be Cut

◈ Diamonds reflect the Light!

You are A Diamond In Process

Your Invitation: You Are A GEM!

Today, Jesus Christ "The Master Jeweler" invites you into a personal relationship with Him! He knows how to clean you off, polish you up and has a plan to brilliantly shine through your life for HIS glory!

"Those who look to him are radiant; their faces are never covered with shame."
Psalm 34:5 NIV

"And the Lord their God will save them on that day as the flock of His people, for they shall be as the [precious] jewels of a crown, lifted high over and shining glitteringly upon His land."
Zechariah 9:16 AMPC

Will you choose to allow Him to enter into your life? He is the King Of Kings, and Lord of Lords. Jesus Christ wants to be the lover of your soul, your companion, your most intimate friend, and closer than your very breath.

If you do not know or have a personal relationship with Jesus Christ, He invites you to do the following:

"That if you confess with your mouth Jesus as Lord, and believe in your heart that God raised Him from the dead, you shall be saved; for with the heart man believes, resulting in righteousness, and with the mouth he confesses, resulting in salvation."

Romans 10:9,10 NAS

If you have fallen away from your relationship with Jesus Christ and you genuinely desire to renew it, then ask for His forgiveness today. He will restore your relationship by making it brand new!

"If we confess our sins, He is faithful and righteous to forgive us our sins and to cleanse us from all unrighteousness.

I John 1:9 NAS

If you would also like to be connected with a local church contact us.

Amen!

Your Next Steps

You have discovered 5 GEMS to become...

UNSTUCK!

For More Resources Go to:

MININGFORGEMS.COM:

◈ For Your FREE Success Road Map

◈ For Your FREE GEM Recap Checklist

◈ To access the additional transforming GEMS

◈ To ask about GEM One-On-One Coaching Availability

◈ To invite the Author to train your team to discover their GEMS

CONTACT: INFO@MININGFORGEMS.COM

571-766-8661

Share YOUR GEM Story!

Help encourage others to become UNSTUCK by sharing your GEM journey with them! You may post at: www.miningforgems.com/mygemstory

For Your Reference List The Names Below:

Tired of Being... Stuck?

Other Books by Michele R. Jones

Your Call To Freedom! ~ Bible Based Tools To
Heal From An Abusive Relationship

(Available in English and Spanish translations)

www.miningforgems.com/GEMS_YCTF

Made in the USA
Middletown, DE
09 December 2017